SHAKESPEARE'S SONNETS

D1392784

The RSC Shakespeare

SHAKESPEARE'S SONNETS

Edited by
Jonathan Bate and Eric Rasmussen

With a Foreword by Fiona Shaw

First published 2011 by
PALGRAVE MACMILLAN
Houndmills, Basingstoke, Hampshire RG21 6XS
Companies and representatives throughout the world

Palgrave Macmillan in the UK is an imprint of Macmillan Publishers Limited,
registered in England, company number 785998, of Houndmills, Basingstoke,
Hampshire RG21 6XS.

Palgrave® and Macmillan® are registered trademarks in the United States,
the United Kingdom, Europe and other countries.

ISBN-13 978–0–230–29041–9 paperback

This book is printed on paper suitable for recycling and made from fully
managed and sustained forest sources.

A catalogue record for this book is available from the British Library.

Printed in China

FOREWORD

Fiona Shaw

Like most people, I found the sonnets hard at school; they seemed to hold some intellectual mystique – to appreciate them I thought one had to be brainy and assumed that all people that lived before us were better at being 'poetical'. That may be true, of course – we shall never know. But the astonishing discovery – if one can get to it – is not that the sonnets are hard or dangerous to our computer minds, but that they hold for us the essence of our struggling emotional lives. Where sentiments have got hijacked by the film companies, and the internet's tools of exposure, where the shared sheep-like feeling of love and loss have become the fodder for formula and romance, Shakespeare's sonnets go on being a handbook of how to survive the interior chaos of love and how to celebrate the exquisite humiliation of being human.

Open this book at any page, you might find:

... precious friends hid in death's dateless night

which is as gloomily relevant today as ever. Or another:

> When in disgrace with Fortune and men's eyes,
> I all alone beweep my outcast state ....

At the centre of this is the existential murmuring that has dogged our simian minds from then to Beckett, or since we were cursed by thought and isolation.

The gentle self-mocking tone seduces us into following on with the story, while the rhythm of the words, the famous iambic plodding, is the heartbeat of the language that lulls us into identification. We are entertained and challenged at the same time; this is what we all feel sometimes, but the recognition is not just here but in the argument through the poem and to the relief of getting somewhere:

> Haply I think on thee and then my state,
> Like to the lark at break of day ...

Shakespeare uses a basic rhythm of a long beat and a short beat, the drum of our thoughts, in which, through a totality of vocabulary, each sonnet works its magic. He surrounds us with a landscape that is emotionally correct for the territory he is investigating. The poems are always spoken to someone, so are never abstractions of the mind. He crunches consonants when he wants the tightness of claustrophobia:

Desiring this man's art and that man's scope

and releases us into 'break of day' – open vowels when letting us go.

The sonnets have a surface of argument that guides us carefully through a troubled interior. Pick another:

No longer mourn for me when I am dead
Than you shall hear the surly sullen bell
Give warning to the world that I am fled
From this vile world with vilest worms to dwell.

Here is all the theatricality of the plays, the extravagance of feeling, but the internal rhymes 'dead', 'fled', 'world' hold the sound of a tolling bell, which stirs the unconscious to a state of mourning.

Death, time and love are sharply intertwined. Ambivalence, the seesaw of our wayward natures and nature itself all play out in this compact totality and are always refracted in the attitude of each poem, sometimes surprisingly opposite in style. The transformative dignity of:

> Let me not to the marriage of true minds
> Admit impediments. Love is not love
> Which alters when it alteration finds

compared to the revulsion of:

> Th'expense of spirit in a waste of shame
> Is lust in action, and till action, lust
> Is perjured, murd'rous, bloody, full of blame.

We are led into the soothing landscape in the gently presented:

> Shall I compare thee to a summer's day?
> Thou art more lovely and more temperate

but the lurking viper of our temporary equilibrium lies in the heart of the poem.

Some sonnets dare to ask the questions that all tortured lovers feel, so that time and love are intertwined:

Being your slave, what should I do but tend
Upon the hours and times of your desires?

Each of us continues to be part of the movement of feeling that, despite its individual tone, is exactly the same down the generations. There is a sinewy tenacity in the way the mind worms in jealousy:

Is it thy will thy image should keep open
My heavy eyelids to the weary night?

right down to the unresolved:

For thee watch I, whilst thou dost wake elsewhere,
From me far off, with others all too near.

Each poem has a consistent vocabulary to guide the reader though the image as it develops. He does some of the work for you; all we have to do is sail with the word and come about when he throws in the volta cutting the argument across with a 'but' or:

Oh no, thy love, though much, is not so great

and reverses the wind of the poem.

Miraculously often written in one draft and apparently learned on one hearing, they are treats that sometimes mock the form of poetry itself:

My mistress' eyes are nothing like the sun,
...
If hairs be wires, black wires grow on her head.

Shakespeare's sonnets give us the impetus required for a meaningful analysis of our foolish selves in love and our difficulty in really communicating with one another.

He uses the 'ifs' and 'buts' of all our conflicting thoughts, and all in the pocketbook size of the sonnet. They are like literary entries in the diary of the human condition. We borrow his words and his rhythm, his hesitancy, his ease with conclusion, and it helps us to do more than merely navigate through the often fraught landscape of love and delight ourselves along the way.

We live in a time where being unable to utter our personal truth seems to hold more integrity. We have become suspicious of words. Shakespeare's sonnets entice us back to a more precise rendering of emotional reality, and they do it with generous and extravagant language. In a sentence he captures the sound and the terror of feeling.

I dip into the sonnets often when performing a Shakespeare play. They are the concentrated form of the stuff that made his plays genius. We and language meet in the sonnets, whether it's comparing someone to a summer's day or worrying about the shore and its image of dragging us screaming into oblivion. He does not ram religion or philosophy down our throats, he merely tells us what it feels like to be human. In fourteen lines he mends an upset, usually by acknowledging that the troubled lover is the cure as well as the cause of the upset. If selected for that 'Desert Island', they would be a perfect choice. They trigger other thoughts, they suggest films and ideas. One can open them up anywhere and just read, and if it takes a while to be allowed to hear the interior then it is time so well spent.

Unique to the writer and unique to each of us who reads them, these sonnets are minted from a language that was contemporary to him, but their quality and precision has overleapt the intervening time.

THE STORY OF THE SONNETS

Jonathan Bate

On 20 May 1609 a publisher called Thomas Thorpe registered his right to publish 'a booke called Shakespeares sonnettes'. A few weeks later, browsing the bookstalls in the yard of London's St Paul's Cathedral, you could have found the little volume and purchased it for sixpence.

Probably the greatest love poems in English literature (though John Donne runs them close), the sonnets introduced to the language such phrases as 'Shall I compare thee to a summer's day?', 'the darling buds of May', 'remembrance of things past' and 'Farewell, thou art too dear for my possessing'. They express almost every phase and every permutation of love, from the first leap of the heart at the sight of your beloved's beauty to the last ache of sorrow and bitterness in the face of death or, worse, betrayal.

Reading the sequence through, there seems to be a story behind it – though, in sharp contrast to Shakespeare's plays, the twists of the plot and the nature of the characters are shadowy and mysterious. The poet begins by addressing a beautiful and high-ranking young man. The youth is in a position of power and the poet in one of supplication. Absence, travel, scandal, melancholy, estrangement and reunion are variously implied. The young man appears to have an affair with the poet's mistress, thus abusing the bond of friendship. Then the poet is discomposed by a rival who wins the patronage of the fair youth with his 'well-refined pen'.

Again and again, the sequence returns to the great battle between love and time. The mood becomes autumnal ('Bare ruined choirs where late the sweet birds sang'). Time is relentless ('Like as the waves make towards the pebbled shore, / So do our minutes hasten to their end'), but the act of writing offers the hope of immortality ('So long as men can breathe or eyes can see, / So long lives this and this gives life to thee').

Then the poet turns his attention from the 'lovely boy' to the 'dark lady'. Dark-complexioned and sexually voracious, she inspires a complex mix of emotions: desire, fondness, self-abnegation, misogyny, a lingering sense of the sour taste that comes after sex ('Th'expense of spirit in a waste of shame / Is lust in action'). One moment the poet is bitter, the next dazzlingly playful, as he parodies conventional love poetry ('My mistress' eyes are nothing like the sun') and puns on the multiple senses of the word that is also his own name: 'Will'.

We think of love sonnets as the most personal of poems. The little book called *Shakespeare's Sonnets* is a source of endless fascination because it seems to be the one work in which its author speaks in his own voice. 'Scorn not the sonnet', William Wordsworth would write two centuries after they were published: 'With this key, Shakespeare unlocked his heart'. So it is that the sonnets are often believed to bear a wholly different relationship to Shakespeare's biography from that of the rest of his literary work. There is, however, no intrinsic reason why a sonnet – a highly artificial literary form – should not be a dramatic performance just as a play is. It may be that for an Elizabethan poet to dash off a sequence of sonnets was a kind of exercise, a proof of artistic skill akin to the work of a composer writing a set of variations on a musical theme.

If Shakespeare could imagine Hamlet and Romeo and Viola, he could also have invented the 'plot' and 'characters' of his sonnets. Robert Browning responded to Wordsworth's claim: 'If so, the less Shakespeare he!' Maybe the sonnets are best read as showpieces of Shakespeare's art, demonstrations of his unsurpassed gift for pinpointing the many moods of love and transforming them into beautiful, memorable language.

We do not know whether the sonnets are dramatic performances written out of sheer zest for feelings and words or whether they are poetic reimaginings of real figures and events. Unlike several contemporary sonneteers, Shakespeare does not name names, save for his own. Because he is so guarded, the circumstances in which the sonnets were created provoked centuries of speculation – about the identity of the 'fair youth' and the 'dark lady', about the extent to which the sonnets are or are not autobiographical, about the sexual orientation they imply.

The young man to whom many of the poems are addressed may or may not be synonymous with the mysterious 'Mr. W. H.' named in the collection's dedication. It is, however, striking that dozens and dozens of male

Elizabethan poets wrote sonnet sequences, but only Shakespeare and a now forgotten poet called Richard Barnfield addressed their poems explicitly to a man. Barnfield wrote in the explicitly homoerotic tradition of ancient Greek pastoral poetry, whereas Shakespeare's sequence emphasizes the spiritual aspects of the poet's love for the fair youth. The only sonnets in the collection where 'Will' is actually in bed with a lover are addressed to the dark lady. The young man's 'thing' (which has been 'pricked out' by nature) is, says the poet in Sonnet 20, 'to my purpose nothing' – though this is supremely ambiguous, since it could mean either that he is not interested in a physical relationship or that the prick serves him in the same way that a woman's 'nothing' (an Elizabethan slang term for the female sexual parts) would serve another man. Taken in their entirety, the sonnets seem to associate heterosexual desire with consummation and disgust, homoerotic attraction with spirituality and an intensity that derives in large measure from the impossibility of consummation. Tempting as it may be to infer Shakespeare's sexuality from this duality, it might be better to read the opposition between dark lady and fair youth as a dramatic device: one is a 'character' representing desire in its sexual manifestation, the other in its idealizing and spiritual.

Besides, many of the poems do not specify the gender of the beloved. 'Let me not to the marriage of true minds / Admit impediments' has long been a favourite for reading at weddings, not least because its language plays on the formal wording of the marriage service ('If any of you know cause, or just impediment, why these two persons should not be joined together in holy Matrimony, speak now or forever hold your peace'). Since it is grouped among the sonnets that appear to address the young man, one might suppose that it would be more fitting for a same-sex civil partnership than a heterosexual wedding. But it is unlikely that Shakespeare ordered the sonnets himself: this one could perfectly well have been written with a woman in mind. There is nothing peculiar or inappropriate about its traditional use.

Precisely because of Shakespeare's refusal to name names or anchor the sonnets strictly in his own experience, readers are free to make the poems their own. The capacity to generate stories and theories and multiple interpretations is part of the magic of this extraordinary collection. Each reader projects into it their own imagined narrative of Shakespeare's experience of love. But what the narrative really reveals is something of our own feelings about love. The sonnets work like love itself by making you want to join your story to that of another. And that, of course, is why they are the greatest of all love poems and why they are still so fresh after four hundred years. When Shakespeare writes 'Let me not to the marriage of true minds / Admit impediments' the two minds that are joined are no longer his and his lover's. When I read the poem, they are mine and my lover's. When you read it, they are yours and your lover's. Scorn not the sonnet, we might say, adapting Wordsworth: with this key Shakespeare unlocks the reader's heart.

SHAKESPEARE'S SONNETS

TO THE ONLY BEGETTER OF
THESE INSUING SONNETS
MR. W. H. ALL HAPPINESS
AND THAT ETERNITY
PROMISED
BY
OUR EVER-LIVING POET
WISHETH
THE WELL-WISHING
ADVENTURER IN
SETTING
FORTH

T. T.

Sonnet 1

FROM fairest creatures we desire increase,
That thereby beauty's rose might never die,
But as the riper should by time decease,
His tender heir might bear his memory:
But thou, contracted to thine own bright eyes,
Feed'st thy light's flame with self-substantial fuel,
Making a famine where abundance lies,
Thyself thy foe, to thy sweet self too cruel.
Thou that art now the world's fresh ornament
And only herald to the gaudy spring,
Within thine own bud buriest thy content
And, tender churl, mak'st waste in niggarding.
    Pity the world, or else this glutton be,
    To eat the world's due, by the grave and thee.

Sonnet 2

When forty winters shall besiege thy brow
And dig deep trenches in thy beauty's field,
Thy youth's proud livery, so gazed on now,
Will be a tattered weed of small worth held:
Then being asked where all thy beauty lies,
Where all the treasure of thy lusty days,
To say within thine own deep-sunken eyes
Were an all-eating shame and thriftless praise.
How much more praise deserved thy beauty's use
If thou couldst answer, 'This fair child of mine
Shall sum my count and make my old excuse',
Proving his beauty by succession thine.
   This were to be new made when thou art old
   And see thy blood warm when thou feel'st it cold.

Sonnet 3

Look in thy glass and tell the face thou viewest
Now is the time that face should form another,
Whose fresh repair if now thou not renewest
Thou dost beguile the world, unbless some mother.
For where is she so fair whose uneared womb
Disdains the tillage of thy husbandry?
Or who is he so fond will be the tomb
Of his self-love, to stop posterity?
Thou art thy mother's glass and she in thee
Calls back the lovely April of her prime:
So thou through windows of thine age shalt see,
Despite of wrinkles, this thy golden time.
   But if thou live remembered not to be,
   Die single and thine image dies with thee.

Sonnet 4

Unthrifty loveliness, why dost thou spend
Upon thyself thy beauty's legacy?
Nature's bequest gives nothing but doth lend,
And being frank she lends to those are free.
Then, beauteous niggard, why dost thou abuse
The bounteous largesse given thee to give?
Profitless usurer, why dost thou use
So great a sum of sums, yet canst not live?
For having traffic with thyself alone,
Thou of thyself thy sweet self dost deceive.
Then how, when nature calls thee to be gone,
What acceptable audit canst thou leave?
   Thy unused beauty must be tombed with thee,
   Which, usèd, lives th'executor to be.

Sonnet 5

Those hours, that with gentle work did frame
The lovely gaze where every eye doth dwell,
Will play the tyrants to the very same
And that unfair which fairly doth excel:
For never-resting time leads summer on
To hideous winter and confounds him there,
Sap checked with frost and lusty leaves quite gone,
Beauty o'ersnowed and bareness everywhere.
Then, were not summer's distillation left
A liquid prisoner pent in walls of glass,
Beauty's effect with beauty were bereft,
Nor it nor no remembrance what it was.
    But flowers distilled, though they with winter meet,
    Lose but their show, their substance still lives sweet.

Sonnet 6

Then let not winter's ragged hand deface
In thee thy summer, ere thou be distilled:
Make sweet some vial; treasure thou some place
With beauty's treasure, ere it be self-killed.
That use is not forbidden usury,
Which happies those that pay the willing loan;
That's for thyself to breed another thee,
Or ten times happier be it ten for one.
Ten times thyself were happier than thou art,
If ten of thine ten times refigured thee.
Then what could death do, if thou shouldst depart,
Leaving thee living in posterity?
    Be not self-willed, for thou art much too fair
    To be death's conquest and make worms thine heir.

Sonnet 7

Lo, in the orient when the gracious light
Lifts up his burning head, each under eye
Doth homage to his new-appearing sight,
Serving with looks his sacred majesty.
And having climbed the steep-up heavenly hill,
Resembling strong youth in his middle age,
Yet mortal looks adore his beauty still,
Attending on his golden pilgrimage.
But when from highmost pitch, with weary car,
Like feeble age he reeleth from the day,
The eyes, fore duteous, now converted are
From his low tract and look another way:
    So thou, thyself outgoing in thy noon,
    Unlooked on diest unless thou get a son.

Sonnet 8

Music to hear, why hear'st thou music sadly?
Sweets with sweets war not, joy delights in joy.
Why lov'st thou that which thou receiv'st not gladly,
Or else receiv'st with pleasure thine annoy?
If the true concord of well-tunèd sounds,
By unions married, do offend thine ear,
They do but sweetly chide thee, who confounds
In singleness the parts that thou shouldst bear.
Mark how one string, sweet husband to another,
Strikes each in each by mutual ordering,
Resembling sire and child and happy mother
Who, all in one, one pleasing note do sing,
    Whose speechless song, being many, seeming one,
    Sings this to thee: 'Thou single wilt prove none.'

Sonnet 9

Is it for fear to wet a widow's eye
That thou consum'st thyself in single life?
Ah, if thou issueless shalt hap to die,
The world will wail thee, like a makeless wife,
The world will be thy widow and still weep
That thou no form of thee hast left behind,
When every private widow well may keep
By children's eyes her husband's shape in mind.
Look what an unthrift in the world doth spend
Shifts but his place, for still the world enjoys it,
But beauty's waste hath in the world an end,
And, kept unused, the user so destroys it.
   No love toward others in that bosom sits
   That on himself such murd'rous shame commits.

Sonnet 10

For shame deny that thou bear'st love to any,
Who for thyself art so unprovident.
Grant, if thou wilt, thou art beloved of many,
But that thou none lov'st is most evident:
For thou art so possessed with murd'rous hate
That gainst thyself thou stick'st not to conspire,
Seeking that beauteous roof to ruinate
Which to repair should be thy chief desire.
O, change thy thought, that I may change my mind.
Shall hate be fairer lodged than gentle love?
Be as thy presence is, gracious and kind,
Or to thyself at least kind-hearted prove.
    Make thee another self, for love of me,
    That beauty still may live in thine or thee.

Sonnet 11

As fast as thou shalt wane, so fast thou grow'st
In one of thine, from that which thou departest,
And that fresh blood which youngly thou bestow'st,
Thou mayst call thine when thou from youth convertest.
Herein lives wisdom, beauty and increase:
Without this, folly, age and cold decay.
If all were minded so, the times should cease,
And threescore year would make the world away.
Let those whom nature hath not made for store,
Harsh, featureless and rude, barrenly perish.
Look whom she best endowed she gave the more,
Which bounteous gift thou shouldst in bounty cherish.
   She carved thee for her seal, and meant thereby
   Thou shouldst print more, not let that copy die.

Sonnet 12

When I do count the clock that tells the time
And see the brave day sunk in hideous night,
When I behold the violet past prime
And sable curls all silvered o'er with white,
When lofty trees I see barren of leaves,
Which erst from heat did canopy the herd,
And summer's green all girded up in sheaves
Borne on the bier with white and bristly beard:
Then of thy beauty do I question make
That thou among the wastes of time must go,
Since sweets and beauties do themselves forsake
And die as fast as they see others grow,
    And nothing gainst Time's scythe can make defence
    Save breed, to brave him when he takes thee hence.

Sonnet 13

O, that you were yourself! But, love, you are
No longer yours than you yourself here live.
Against this coming end you should prepare
And your sweet semblance to some other give.
So should that beauty which you hold in lease
Find no determination: then you were
Yourself again after yourself's decease,
When your sweet issue your sweet form should bear.
Who lets so fair a house fall to decay,
Which husbandry in honour might uphold
Against the stormy gusts of winter's day
And barren rage of death's eternal cold?
  O, none but unthrifts! Dear my love, you know
  You had a father: let your son say so.

Sonnet 14

Not from the stars do I my judgement pluck
And yet methinks I have astronomy,
But not to tell of good or evil luck,
Of plagues, of dearths, or seasons' quality,
Nor can I fortune to brief minutes tell,
Pointing to each his thunder, rain and wind,
Or say with princes if it shall go well,
By oft predict that I in heaven find.
But from thine eyes my knowledge I derive,
And, constant stars, in them I read such art
As truth and beauty shall together thrive,
If from thyself to store thou wouldst convert:
    Or else of thee this I prognosticate,
    Thy end is truth's and beauty's doom and date.

Sonnet 15

When I consider everything that grows
Holds in perfection but a little moment,
That this huge stage presenteth nought but shows
Whereon the stars in secret influence comment:
When I perceive that men as plants increase,
Cheerèd and checked ev'n by the selfsame sky,
Vaunt in their youthful sap, at height decrease,
And wear their brave state out of memory:
Then the conceit of this inconstant stay
Sets you most rich in youth before my sight,
Where wasteful time debateth with decay
To change your day of youth to sullied night,
    And all in war with Time for love of you,
    As he takes from you, I engraft you new.

Sonnet 16

But wherefore do not you a mightier way
Make war upon this bloody tyrant, Time?
And fortify yourself in your decay
With means more blessèd than my barren rhyme?
Now stand you on the top of happy hours,
And many maiden gardens, yet unset,
With virtuous wish would bear your living flowers,
Much liker than your painted counterfeit:
So should the lines of life that life repair,
Which this, Time's pencil, or my pupil pen,
Neither in inward worth nor outward fair,
Can make you live yourself in eyes of men.
   To give away yourself keeps yourself still,
    And you must live, drawn by your own sweet skill.

Sonnet 17

Who will believe my verse in time to come
If it were filled with your most high deserts?
Though yet, heaven knows, it is but as a tomb
Which hides your life and shows not half your parts.
If I could write the beauty of your eyes
And in fresh numbers number all your graces,
The age to come would say, 'This poet lies:
Such heavenly touches ne'er touched earthly faces.'
So should my papers, yellowed with their age,
Be scorned like old men of less truth than tongue,
And your true rights be termed a poet's rage
And stretchèd metre of an antique song.
    But were some child of yours alive that time,
      You should live twice — in it and in my rhyme.

Sonnet 18

Shall I compare thee to a summer's day?
Thou art more lovely and more temperate.
Rough winds do shake the darling buds of May,
And summer's lease hath all too short a date.
Sometime too hot the eye of heaven shines,
And often is his gold complexion dimmed,
And every fair from fair sometime declines,
By chance or nature's changing course untrimmed:
But thy eternal summer shall not fade
Nor lose possession of that fair thou ow'st,
Nor shall death brag thou wand'rest in his shade,
When in eternal lines to time thou grow'st.
   So long as men can breathe or eyes can see,
   So long lives this and this gives life to thee.

Sonnet 19

Devouring Time, blunt thou the lion's paws,
And make the earth devour her own sweet brood,
Pluck the keen teeth from the fierce tiger's jaws
And burn the long-lived phoenix in her blood,
Make glad and sorry seasons as thou fleet'st
And do whate'er thou wilt, swift-footed Time,
To the wide world and all her fading sweets.
But I forbid thee one most heinous crime:
O, carve not with thy hours my love's fair brow,
Nor draw no lines there with thine antique pen.
Him in thy course untainted do allow
For beauty's pattern to succeeding men.
   Yet do thy worst, old Time: despite thy wrong,
   My love shall in my verse ever live young.

Sonnet 20

A woman's face with Nature's own hand painted
Hast thou, the master-mistress of my passion,
A woman's gentle heart, but not acquainted
With shifting change as is false women's fashion,
An eye more bright than theirs, less false in rolling,
Gilding the object whereupon it gazeth:
A man in hue, all hues in his controlling,
Which steals men's eyes and women's souls amazeth.
And for a woman wert thou first created,
Till Nature as she wrought thee fell a-doting,
And by addition me of thee defeated
By adding one thing to my purpose nothing.
   But since she pricked thee out for women's pleasure,
   Mine be thy love and thy love's use their treasure.

Sonnet 21

So is it not with me as with that Muse,
Stirred by a painted beauty to his verse,
Who heaven itself for ornament doth use
And every fair with his fair doth rehearse,
Making a couplement of proud compare
With sun and moon, with earth and sea's rich gems,
With April's first-born flowers and all things rare
That heaven's air in this huge rondure hems.
O let me, true in love, but truly write,
And then believe me, my love is as fair
As any mother's child, though not so bright
As those gold candles fixed in heaven's air.
  Let them say more that like of hearsay well:
  I will not praise that purpose not to sell.

Sonnet 22

My glass shall not persuade me I am old,
So long as youth and thou are of one date,
But when in thee time's furrows I behold,
Then look I death my days should expiate.
For all that beauty that doth cover thee
Is but the seemly raiment of my heart,
Which in thy breast doth live, as thine in me:
How can I then be elder than thou art?
O, therefore, love, be of thyself so wary
As I, not for myself, but for thee will,
Bearing thy heart, which I will keep so chary
As tender nurse her babe from faring ill.
    Presume not on thy heart when mine is slain:
    Thou gav'st me thine, not to give back again.

Sonnet 23

As an unperfect actor on the stage,
Who with his fear is put besides his part,
Or some fierce thing replete with too much rage,
Whose strength's abundance weakens his own heart,
So I, for fear of trust, forget to say
The perfect ceremony of love's rite,
And in mine own love's strength seem to decay,
O'ercharged with burden of mine own love's might.
O, let my books be then the eloquence
And dumb presagers of my speaking breast,
Who plead for love and look for recompense,
More than that tongue that more hath more expressed.
   O, learn to read what silent love hath writ:
   To hear with eyes belongs to love's fine wit.

Sonnet 24

Mine eye hath played the painter and hath stelled
Thy beauty's form in table of my heart,
My body is the frame wherein 'tis held
And perspective it is best painter's art.
For through the painter must you see his skill
To find where your true image pictured lies,
Which in my bosom's shop is hanging still,
That hath his windows glazèd with thine eyes.
Now see what good turns eyes for eyes have done:
Mine eyes have drawn thy shape and thine for me
Are windows to my breast, wherethrough the sun
Delights to peep, to gaze therein on thee.
    Yet eyes this cunning want to grace their art:
    They draw but what they see, know not the heart.

Sonnet 25

Let those who are in favour with their stars
Of public honour and proud titles boast,
Whilst I, whom fortune of such triumph bars,
Unlooked for joy in that I honour most.
Great princes' favourites their fair leaves spread
But as the marigold at the sun's eye,
And in themselves their pride lies burièd,
For at a frown they in their glory die.
The painful warrior famousèd for might,
After a thousand victories once foiled,
Is from the book of honour razèd quite
And all the rest forgot for which he toiled.
   Then happy I, that love and am beloved
   Where I may not remove nor be removed.

Sonnet 26

Lord of my love, to whom in vassalage
Thy merit hath my duty strongly knit,
To thee I send this written ambassage
To witness duty, not to show my wit.
Duty so great, which wit so poor as mine
May make seem bare, in wanting words to show it,
But that I hope some good conceit of thine
In thy soul's thought, all naked, will bestow it,
Till whatsoever star that guides my moving
Points on me graciously with fair aspect
And puts apparel on my tattered loving
To show me worthy of thy sweet respect.
    Then may I dare to boast how I do love thee:
    Till then not show my head where thou mayst prove me.

Sonnet 27

Weary with toil, I haste me to my bed,
The dear repose for limbs with travel tired,
But then begins a journey in my head,
To work my mind, when body's work's expired:
For then my thoughts, from far where I abide,
Intend a zealous pilgrimage to thee,
And keep my drooping eyelids open wide,
Looking on darkness which the blind do see,
Save that my soul's imaginary sight
Presents thy shadow to my sightless view,
Which, like a jewel hung in ghastly night,
Makes black night beauteous and her old face new.
  Lo, thus, by day my limbs, by night my mind,
    For thee and for myself no quiet find.

Sonnet 28

How can I then return in happy plight
That am debarred the benefit of rest,
When day's oppression is not eased by night,
But day by night and night by day oppressed?
And each, though enemies to either's reign,
Do in consent shake hands to torture me,
The one by toil, the other to complain
How far I toil, still further off from thee.
I tell the day, to please him thou art bright
And dost him grace when clouds do blot the heaven:
So flatter I the swart-complexioned night,
When sparkling stars twire not thou gild'st the even.
    But day doth daily draw my sorrows longer,
        And night doth nightly make grief's length seem stronger.

Sonnet 29

When in disgrace with Fortune and men's eyes,
I all alone beweep my outcast state
And trouble deaf heaven with my bootless cries
And look upon myself and curse my fate,
Wishing me like to one more rich in hope,
Featured like him, like him with friends possessed,
Desiring this man's art and that man's scope,
With what I most enjoy contented least:
Yet in these thoughts myself almost despising,
Haply I think on thee and then my state,
Like to the lark at break of day arising,
From sullen earth sings hymns at heaven's gate,
 For thy sweet love remembered such wealth brings
 That then I scorn to change my state with kings.

Sonnet 30

When to the sessions of sweet silent thought
I summon up remembrance of things past,
I sigh the lack of many a thing I sought
And with old woes new wail my dear time's waste.
Then can I drown an eye, unused to flow,
For precious friends hid in death's dateless night,
And weep afresh love's long since cancelled woe,
And moan th'expense of many a vanished sight.
Then can I grieve at grievances foregone,
And heavily from woe to woe tell o'er
The sad account of fore-bemoanèd moan,
Which I new pay as if not paid before.
   But if the while I think on thee, dear friend,
   All losses are restored and sorrows end.

Sonnet 31

Thy bosom is endearèd with all hearts,
Which I by lacking have supposèd dead,
And there reigns love and all love's loving parts
And all those friends which I thought burièd.
How many a holy and obsequious tear
Hath dear religious love stol'n from mine eye
As interest of the dead, which now appear
But things removed that hidden in there lie.
Thou art the grave where buried love doth live,
Hung with the trophies of my lovers gone,
Who all their parts of me to thee did give:
That due of many now is thine alone.
   Their images I loved I view in thee,
    And thou, all they, hast all the all of me.

Sonnet 32

If thou survive my well-contented day,
When that churl death my bones with dust shall cover,
And shalt by fortune once more resurvey
These poor rude lines of thy deceasèd lover,
Compare them with the bett'ring of the time,
And though they be outstripped by every pen,
Reserve them for my love, not for their rhyme,
Exceeded by the height of happier men.
O, then vouchsafe me but this loving thought:
'Had my friend's Muse grown with this growing age,
A dearer birth than this his love had brought
To march in ranks of better equipage,
    But since he died and poets better prove,
    Theirs for their style I'll read, his for his love.'

Sonnet 33

Full many a glorious morning have I seen
Flatter the mountain tops with sovereign eye,
Kissing with golden face the meadows green,
Gilding pale streams with heavenly alchemy,
Anon permit the basest clouds to ride
With ugly rack on his celestial face,
And from the forlorn world his visage hide,
Stealing unseen to west with this disgrace:
Even so my sun one early morn did shine
With all-triumphant splendour on my brow:
But out, alack, he was but one hour mine,
The region cloud hath masked him from me now.
   Yet him for this my love no whit disdaineth:
   Suns of the world may stain when heaven's sun staineth.

Sonnet 34

Why didst thou promise such a beauteous day
And make me travel forth without my cloak,
To let base clouds o'ertake me in my way,
Hiding thy brav'ry in their rotten smoke?
'Tis not enough that through the cloud thou break
To dry the rain on my storm-beaten face,
For no man well of such a salve can speak
That heals the wound and cures not the disgrace.
Nor can thy shame give physic to my grief:
Though thou repent, yet I have still the loss.
Th'offender's sorrow lends but weak relief
To him that bears the strong offence's cross.
    Ah, but those tears are pearl, which thy love sheds,
    And they are rich and ransom all ill deeds.

Sonnet 35

No more be grieved at that which thou hast done:
Roses have thorns and silver fountains mud,
Clouds and eclipses stain both moon and sun,
And loathsome canker lives in sweetest bud.
All men make faults and even I in this,
Authorizing thy trespass with compare,
Myself corrupting, salving thy amiss,
Excusing thy sins more than thy sins are:
For to thy sensual fault I bring in sense —
Thy adverse party is thy advocate —
And gainst myself a lawful plea commence.
Such civil war is in my love and hate
    That I an accessory needs must be
    To that sweet thief which sourly robs from me.

Sonnet 36

Let me confess that we two must be twain,
Although our undivided loves are one:
So shall those blots that do with me remain,
Without thy help by me be borne alone.
In our two loves there is but one respect,
Though in our lives a separable spite,
Which though it alter not love's sole effect,
Yet doth it steal sweet hours from love's delight.
I may not evermore acknowledge thee,
Lest my bewailèd guilt should do thee shame,
Nor thou with public kindness honour me,
Unless thou take that honour from thy name.
　　But do not so: I love thee in such sort
　　As, thou being mine, mine is thy good report.

Sonnet 37

As a decrepit father takes delight
To see his active child do deeds of youth,
So I, made lame by Fortune's dearest spite,
Take all my comfort of thy worth and truth.
For whether beauty, birth or wealth or wit,
Or any of these all or all or more,
Entitled in thy parts do crownèd sit,
I make my love engrafted to this store:
So then I am not lame, poor, nor despised,
Whilst that this shadow doth such substance give
That I in thy abundance am sufficed
And by a part of all thy glory live.
    Look what is best, that best I wish in thee.
    This wish I have: then ten times happy me.

Sonnet 38

How can my Muse want subject to invent,
While thou dost breathe, that pour'st into my verse
Thine own sweet argument, too excellent
For every vulgar paper to rehearse?
O, give thyself the thanks, if aught in me
Worthy perusal stand against thy sight,
For who's so dumb that cannot write to thee,
When thou thyself dost give invention light?
Be thou the tenth Muse, ten times more in worth
Than those old nine which rhymers invocate,
And he that calls on thee, let him bring forth
Eternal numbers to outlive long date.
   If my slight Muse do please these curious days,
     The pain be mine, but thine shall be the praise.

Sonnet 39

O, how thy worth with manners may I sing,
When thou art all the better part of me?
What can mine own praise to mine own self bring?
And what is't but mine own when I praise thee?
Even for this let us divided live,
And our dear love lose name of single one,
That by this separation I may give
That due to thee which thou deserv'st alone.
O absence, what a torment wouldst thou prove,
Were it not thy sour leisure gave sweet leave
To entertain the time with thoughts of love,
Which time and thoughts so sweetly dost deceive,
   And that thou teachest how to make one twain
   By praising him here who doth hence remain.

Sonnet 40

Take all my loves, my love, yea, take them all:
What hast thou then more than thou hadst before?
No love, my love, that thou mayst true love call:
All mine was thine before thou hadst this more.
Then if for my love thou my love receivest,
I cannot blame thee for my love thou usest.
But yet be blamed, if thou this self deceivest
By wilful taste of what thyself refusest.
I do forgive thy robb'ry, gentle thief,
Although thou steal thee all my poverty:
And yet love knows it is a greater grief
To bear love's wrong than hate's known injury.
    Lascivious grace, in whom all ill well shows,
    Kill me with spites, yet we must not be foes.

Sonnet 41

Those pretty wrongs that liberty commits
When I am sometime absent from thy heart,
Thy beauty and thy years full well befits,
For still temptation follows where thou art.
Gentle thou art and therefore to be won,
Beauteous thou art, therefore to be assailed.
And when a woman woos, what woman's son
Will sourly leave her till he have prevailed?
Ay me, but yet thou mightst my seat forbear
And chide thy beauty and thy straying youth,
Who lead thee in their riot even there
Where thou art forced to break a two-fold truth:
    Hers by thy beauty tempting her to thee,
    Thine by thy beauty being false to me.

Sonnet 42

That thou hast her, it is not all my grief,
And yet it may be said I loved her dearly,
That she hath thee is of my wailing chief,
A loss in love that touches me more nearly.
Loving offenders, thus I will excuse ye:
Thou dost love her, because thou knowst I love her,
And for my sake even so doth she abuse me,
Suff'ring my friend for my sake to approve her.
If I lose thee, my loss is my love's gain,
And losing her, my friend hath found that loss:
Both find each other and I lose both twain,
And both for my sake lay on me this cross.
   But here's the joy: my friend and I are one.
   Sweet flatt'ry! Then she loves but me alone.

Sonnet 43

When most I wink, then do mine eyes best see,
For all the day they view things unrespected,
But when I sleep, in dreams they look on thee
And, darkly bright, are bright in dark directed.
Then thou, whose shadow shadows doth make bright,
How would thy shadow's form form happy show
To the clear day with thy much clearer light,
When to unseeing eyes thy shade shines so?
How would, I say, mine eyes be blessèd made
By looking on thee in the living day,
When in dead night thy fair imperfect shade
Through heavy sleep on sightless eyes doth stay?
    All days are nights to see till I see thee,
    And nights bright days when dreams do show thee me.

Sonnet 44

If the dull substance of my flesh were thought,
Injurious distance should not stop my way,
For then despite of space I would be brought,
From limits far remote, where thou dost stay.
No matter then, although my foot did stand
Upon the farthest earth removed from thee,
For nimble thought can jump both sea and land
As soon as think the place where he would be.
But ah, thought kills me that I am not thought,
To leap large lengths of miles when thou art gone,
But that so much of earth and water wrought,
I must attend time's leisure with my moan,
    Receiving naught by elements so slow
    But heavy tears, badges of either's woe.

Sonnet 45

The other two, slight air and purging fire,
Are both with thee, wherever I abide:
The first my thought, the other my desire,
These present-absent with swift motion slide.
For when these quicker elements are gone
In tender embassy of love to thee,
My life, being made of four, with two alone
Sinks down to death, oppressed with melancholy,
Until life's composition be recured
By those swift messengers returned from thee,
Who even but now come back again, assured
Of thy fair health, recounting it to me.
   This told, I joy — but then no longer glad,
   I send them back again and straight grow sad.

Sonnet 46

Mine eye and heart are at a mortal war
How to divide the conquest of thy sight:
Mine eye my heart thy picture's sight would bar,
My heart mine eye the freedom of that right.
My heart doth plead that thou in him dost lie —
A closet never pierced with crystal eyes —
But the defendant doth that plea deny
And says in him thy fair appearance lies.
To 'cide this title is empanellèd
A quest of thoughts, all tenants to the heart,
And by their verdict is determinèd
The clear eye's moiety and the dear heart's part,
   As thus: mine eye's due is thy outward part,
    And my heart's right thy inward love of heart.

Sonnet 47

Betwixt mine eye and heart a league is took,
And each doth good turns now unto the other:
When that mine eye is famished for a look,
Or heart in love with sighs himself doth smother,
With my love's picture then my eye doth feast
And to the painted banquet bids my heart.
Another time mine eye is my heart's guest
And in his thoughts of love doth share a part.
So, either by thy picture or my love,
Thyself away are present still with me,
For thou not further than my thoughts canst move,
And I am still with them and they with thee.
    Or, if they sleep, thy picture in my sight
    Awakes my heart to heart's and eye's delight.

Sonnet 48

How careful was I, when I took my way,
Each trifle under truest bars to thrust,
That to my use it might unusèd stay
From hands of falsehood, in sure wards of trust.
But thou, to whom my jewels trifles are,
Most worthy comfort, now my greatest grief,
Thou, best of dearest and mine only care,
Art left the prey of every vulgar thief.
Thee have I not locked up in any chest,
Save where thou art not, though I feel thou art,
Within the gentle closure of my breast,
From whence at pleasure thou mayst come and part:
    And even thence thou wilt be stol'n, I fear,
    For truth proves thievish for a prize so dear.

Sonnet 49

Against that time, if ever that time come,
When I shall see thee frown on my defects,
When as thy love hath cast his utmost sum,
Called to that audit by advised respects —
Against that time when thou shalt strangely pass
And scarcely greet me with that sun thine eye,
When love, converted from the thing it was,
Shall reasons find of settled gravity —
Against that time do I ensconce me here
Within the knowledge of mine own desert,
And this my hand against myself uprear
To guard the lawful reasons on thy part:
    To leave poor me thou hast the strength of laws,
    Since why to love I can allege no cause.

Sonnet 50

How heavy do I journey on the way,
When what I seek, my weary travel's end,
Doth teach that ease and that repose to say,
'Thus far the miles are measured from thy friend.'
The beast that bears me, tirèd with my woe,
Plods dully on, to bear that weight in me,
As if by some instinct the wretch did know
His rider loved not speed, being made from thee:
The bloody spur cannot provoke him on
That sometimes anger thrusts into his hide,
Which heavily he answers with a groan,
More sharp to me than spurring to his side,
    For that same groan doth put this in my mind:
    My grief lies onward and my joy behind.

Sonnet 51

Thus can my love excuse the slow offence
Of my dull bearer when from thee I speed:
From where thou art why should I haste me thence?
Till I return, of posting is no need.
O, what excuse will my poor beast then find,
When swift extremity can seem but slow?
Then should I spur, though mounted on the wind:
In wingèd speed no motion shall I know.
Then can no horse with my desire keep pace:
Therefore desire, of perfects love being made,
Shall neigh — no dull flesh — in his fiery race,
But love, for love, thus shall excuse my jade,
　　Since from thee going he went wilful-slow,
　　Towards thee I'll run and give him leave to go.

Sonnet 52

So am I as the rich, whose blessèd key
Can bring him to his sweet up-lockèd treasure,
The which he will not ev'ry hour survey,
For blunting the fine point of seldom pleasure.
Therefore are feasts so solemn and so rare,
Since, seldom coming, in the long year set
Like stones of worth they thinly placèd are,
Or captain jewels in the carcanet.
So is the time that keeps you as my chest,
Or as the wardrobe which the robe doth hide,
To make some special instant special blest
By new unfolding his imprisoned pride.
    Blessèd are you, whose worthiness gives scope,
    Being had, to triumph, being lacked, to hope.

Sonnet 53

What is your substance, whereof are you made,
That millions of strange shadows on you tend?
Since every one hath, every one, one shade,
And you, but one, can every shadow lend.
Describe Adonis, and the counterfeit
Is poorly imitated after you.
On Helen's cheek all art of beauty set,
And you in Grecian tires are painted new.
Speak of the spring and foison of the year:
The one doth shadow of your beauty show,
The other as your bounty doth appear,
And you in every blessèd shape we know.
    In all external grace you have some part,
    But you like none, none you, for constant heart.

Sonnet 54

O, how much more doth beauty beauteous seem
By that sweet ornament which truth doth give.
The rose looks fair, but fairer we it deem
For that sweet odour which doth in it live.
The canker blooms have full as deep a dye
As the perfumèd tincture of the roses,
Hang on such thorns and play as wantonly
When summer's breath their maskèd buds discloses:
But, for their virtue only is their show,
They live unwooed and unrespected fade,
Die to themselves. Sweet roses do not so:
Of their sweet deaths are sweetest odours made.
   And so of you, beauteous and lovely youth,
    When that shall fade, my verse distils your truth.

Sonnet 55

Not marble nor the gilded monuments
Of princes shall outlive this powerful rhyme,
But you shall shine more bright in these contents
Than unswept stone besmeared with sluttish time.
When wasteful war shall statues overturn,
And broils root out the work of masonry,
Nor Mars his sword, nor war's quick fire shall burn
The living record of your memory.
Gainst death and all oblivious enmity
Shall you pace forth, your praise shall still find room
Even in the eyes of all posterity
That wear this world out to the ending doom.
  So, till the judgement that yourself arise,
  You live in this, and dwell in lovers' eyes.

Sonnet 56

Sweet love, renew thy force. Be it not said
Thy edge should blunter be than appetite,
Which but today by feeding is allayed,
Tomorrow sharpened in his former might.
So love, be thou, although today thou fill
Thy hungry eyes even till they wink with fullness,
Tomorrow see again and do not kill
The spirit of love with a perpetual dullness.
Let this sad int'rim like the ocean be
Which parts the shore, where two contracted new
Come daily to the banks, that, when they see
Return of love, more blest may be the view:
    Or call it winter, which being full of care
    Makes summer's welcome thrice more wished, more rare.

Sonnet 57

Being your slave, what should I do but tend
Upon the hours and times of your desire?
I have no precious time at all to spend,
Nor services to do, till you require.
Nor dare I chide the world-without-end hour
Whilst I, my sovereign, watch the clock for you,
Nor think the bitterness of absence sour
When you have bid your servant once adieu.
Nor dare I question with my jealous thought
Where you may be, or your affairs suppose,
But, like a sad slave, stay and think of nought
Save where you are how happy you make those.
   So true a fool is love that in your Will,
   Though you do anything, he thinks no ill.

Sonnet 58

That god forbid, that made me first your slave,
I should in thought control your times of pleasure,
Or at your hand th'account of hours to crave,
Being your vassal, bound to stay your leisure.
O, let me suffer, being at your beck,
Th'imprisoned absence of your liberty,
And patience tame to sufferance, bide each check
Without accusing you of injury.
Be where you list, your charter is so strong
That you yourself may privilege your time
To what you will: to you it doth belong
Yourself to pardon of self-doing crime.
　I am to wait, though waiting so be hell,
　Not blame your pleasure, be it ill or well.

Sonnet 59

If there be nothing new, but that which is
Hath been before, how are our brains beguiled,
Which, labouring for invention, bear amiss
The second burden of a former child.
O, that record could with a backward look,
Even of five hundred courses of the sun,
Show me your image in some antique book,
Since mind at first in character was done,
That I might see what the old world could say
To this composèd wonder of your frame:
Whether we are mended, or whe'er better they,
Or whether revolution be the same.
 O, sure I am the wits of former days
 To subjects worse have given admiring praise.

Sonnet 60

Like as the waves make towards the pebbled shore,
So do our minutes hasten to their end,
Each changing place with that which goes before,
In sequent toil all forwards do contend.
Nativity, once in the main of light,
Crawls to maturity, wherewith being crowned,
Crooked eclipses gainst his glory fight,
And Time that gave doth now his gift confound.
Time doth transfix the flourish set on youth
And delves the parallels in beauty's brow,
Feeds on the rarities of nature's truth,
And nothing stands but for his scythe to mow.
　　And yet to times in hope my verse shall stand,
　　Praising thy worth, despite his cruel hand.

Sonnet 61

Is it thy will thy image should keep open
My heavy eyelids to the weary night?
Dost thou desire my slumbers should be broken,
While shadows like to thee do mock my sight?
Is it thy spirit that thou send'st from thee
So far from home into my deeds to pry,
To find out shames and idle hours in me,
The scope and tenure of thy jealousy?
O no, thy love, though much, is not so great:
It is my love that keeps mine eye awake,
Mine own true love that doth my rest defeat
To play the watchman ever for thy sake.
   For thee watch I, whilst thou dost wake elsewhere,
   From me far off, with others all too near.

Sonnet 62

Sin of self-love possesseth all mine eye
And all my soul and all my every part,
And for this sin there is no remedy,
It is so grounded inward in my heart.
Methinks no face so gracious is as mine,
No shape so true, no truth of such account,
And for myself mine own worth do define,
As I all other in all worths surmount.
But when my glass shows me myself indeed,
Beated and chopped with tanned antiquity,
Mine own self-love quite contrary I read:
Self so self-loving were iniquity.
    'Tis thee, my self, that for myself I praise,
    Painting my age with beauty of thy days.

Sonnet 63

Against my love shall be as I am now
With Time's injurious hand crushed and o'er-worn,
When hours have drained his blood and filed his brow
With lines and wrinkles, when his youthful morn
Hath travelled on to age's steepy night,
And all those beauties whereof now he's king
Are vanishing, or vanished, out of sight,
Stealing away the treasure of his spring:
For such a time do I now fortify
Against confounding age's cruel knife,
That he shall never cut from memory
My sweet love's beauty, though my lover's life.
    His beauty shall in these black lines be seen,
    And they shall live and he in them still green.

Sonnet 64

When I have seen by Time's fell hand defaced
The rich proud cost of outworn buried age,
When sometime lofty towers I see down-razed
And brass eternal slave to mortal rage,
When I have seen the hungry ocean gain
Advantage on the kingdom of the shore,
And the firm soil win of the wat'ry main,
Increasing store with loss and loss with store,
When I have seen such interchange of state,
Or state itself confounded to decay,
Ruin hath taught me thus to ruminate
That Time will come and take my love away.
   This thought is as a death, which cannot choose
   But weep to have that which it fears to lose.

Sonnet 65

Since brass nor stone nor earth nor boundless sea,
But sad mortality o'er-sways their power,
How with this rage shall beauty hold a plea,
Whose action is no stronger than a flower?
O, how shall summer's honey breath hold out
Against the wrackful siege of batt'ring days,
When rocks impregnable are not so stout,
Nor gates of steel so strong, but time decays?
O fearful meditation! Where, alack,
Shall Time's best jewel from Time's chest lie hid?
Or what strong hand can hold his swift foot back,
Or who his spoil of beauty can forbid?
    O none, unless this miracle have might,
    That in black ink my love may still shine bright.

Sonnet 66

Tired with all these, for restful death I cry,
As to behold desert a beggar born,
And needy nothing trimmed in jollity,
And purest faith unhappily forsworn,
And gilded honour shamefully misplaced,
And maiden virtue rudely strumpeted,
And right perfection wrongfully disgraced,
And strength by limping sway disablèd,
And art made tongue-tied by authority,
And folly doctor-like controlling skill,
And simple truth miscalled simplicity,
And captive good attending captain ill.
  Tired with all these, from these would I be gone,
  Save that to die I leave my love alone.

Sonnet 67

Ah, wherefore with infection should he live,
And with his presence grace impiety,
That sin by him advantage should achieve
And lace itself with his society?
Why should false painting imitate his cheek
And steal dead seeing of his living hue?
Why should poor beauty indirectly seek
Roses of shadow, since his rose is true?
Why should he live, now Nature bankrupt is,
Beggared of blood to blush through lively veins,
For she hath no exchequer now but his,
And, proud of many, lives upon his gains?
    O, him she stores, to show what wealth she had
    In days long since, before these last so bad.

Sonnet 68

Thus is his cheek the map of days outworn,
When beauty lived and died as flowers do now,
Before these bastard signs of fair were born
Or durst inhabit on a living brow,
Before the golden tresses of the dead,
The right of sepulchres, were shorn away,
To live a second life on second head,
Ere beauty's dead fleece made another gay:
In him those holy antique hours are seen,
Without all ornament, itself and true,
Making no summer of another's green,
Robbing no old to dress his beauty new,
    And him as for a map doth Nature store,
      To show false Art what beauty was of yore.

Sonnet 69

Those parts of thee that the world's eye doth view
Want nothing that the thought of hearts can mend:
All tongues, the voice of souls, give thee that due,
Utt'ring bare truth, even so as foes commend.
Thy outward thus with outward praise is crowned,
But those same tongues that give thee so thine own
In other accents do this praise confound
By seeing farther than the eye hath shown.
They look into the beauty of thy mind,
And that, in guess, they measure by thy deeds.
Then, churls, their thoughts, although their eyes were kind,
To thy fair flower add the rank smell of weeds:
   But why thy odour matcheth not thy show,
   The soil is this, that thou dost common grow.

Sonnet 70

That thou art blamed shall not be thy defect,
For slander's mark was ever yet the fair:
The ornament of beauty is suspect,
A crow that flies in heaven's sweetest air.
So thou be good, slander doth but approve
Thy worth the greater, being wooed oft-time:
For canker vice the sweetest buds doth love,
And thou present'st a pure unstainèd prime.
Thou hast passed by the ambush of young days,
Either not assailed or victor being charged:
Yet this thy praise cannot be so thy praise,
To tie up envy evermore enlarged.
  If some suspect of ill masked not thy show,
  Then thou alone kingdoms of hearts shouldst owe.

Sonnet 71

No longer mourn for me when I am dead
Than you shall hear the surly sullen bell
Give warning to the world that I am fled
From this vile world with vilest worms to dwell.
Nay, if you read this line, remember not
The hand that writ it, for I love you so
That I in your sweet thoughts would be forgot,
If thinking on me then should make you woe.
O, if, I say, you look upon this verse
When I perhaps compounded am with clay,
Do not so much as my poor name rehearse,
But let your love even with my life decay,
   Lest the wise world should look into your moan
   And mock you with me after I am gone.

Sonnet 72

O, lest the world should task you to recite
What merit lived in me, that you should love
After my death, dear love, forget me quite,
For you in me can nothing worthy prove,
Unless you would devise some virtuous lie
To do more for me than mine own desert
And hang more praise upon deceasèd I
Than niggard truth would willingly impart.
O, lest your true love may seem false in this,
That you for love speak well of me untrue,
My name be buried where my body is
And live no more to shame nor me nor you.
   For I am shamed by that which I bring forth,
    And so should you, to love things nothing worth.

Sonnet 73

That time of year thou mayst in me behold
When yellow leaves, or none, or few, do hang
Upon those boughs which shake against the cold,
Bare ruined choirs, where late the sweet birds sang.
In me thou see'st the twilight of such day
As after sunset fadeth in the west,
Which by and by black night doth take away,
Death's second self, that seals up all in rest.
In me thou see'st the glowing of such fire
That on the ashes of his youth doth lie,
As the death-bed whereon it must expire,
Consumed with that which it was nourished by.
    This thou perceiv'st, which makes thy love more strong
    To love that well which thou must leave ere long.

Sonnet 74

But be contented when that fell arrest
Without all bail shall carry me away:
My life hath in this line some interest,
Which for memorial still with thee shall stay.
When thou reviewest this, thou dost review
The very part was consecrate to thee.
The earth can have but earth, which is his due:
My spirit is thine, the better part of me.
So then thou hast but lost the dregs of life,
The prey of worms, my body being dead,
The coward conquest of a wretch's knife,
Too base of thee to be rememberèd.
   The worth of that is that which it contains,
   And that is this, and this with thee remains.

Sonnet 75

So are you to my thoughts as food to life
Or as sweet-seasoned showers are to the ground,
And for the peace of you I hold such strife
As 'twixt a miser and his wealth is found:
Now proud as an enjoyer and anon
Doubting the filching age will steal his treasure,
Now counting best to be with you alone,
Then bettered that the world may see my pleasure,
Sometime all full with feasting on your sight,
And by and by clean starvèd for a look,
Possessing or pursuing no delight,
Save what is had or must from you be took.
  Thus do I pine and surfeit day by day,
  Or gluttoning on all, or all away.

Sonnet 76

Why is my verse so barren of new pride?
So far from variation or quick change?
Why with the time do I not glance aside
To new-found methods and to compounds strange?
Why write I still all one, ever the same,
And keep invention in a noted weed,
That every word doth almost tell my name,
Showing their birth and where they did proceed?
O know, sweet love, I always write of you,
And you and love are still my argument:
So all my best is dressing old words new,
Spending again what is already spent,
    For as the sun is daily new and old,
    So is my love still telling what is told.

Sonnet 77

Thy glass will show thee how thy beauties wear,
Thy dial how thy precious minutes waste,
The vacant leaves thy mind's imprint will bear,
And of this book this learning mayst thou taste.
The wrinkles which thy glass will truly show
Of mouthèd graves will give thee memory,
Thou by thy dial's shady stealth mayst know
Time's thievish progress to eternity.
Look what thy memory cannot contain
Commit to these waste blanks and thou shalt find
Those children nursed, delivered from thy brain,
To take a new acquaintance of thy mind.
    These offices, so oft as thou wilt look,
      Shall profit thee and much enrich thy book.

Sonnet 78

So oft have I invoked thee for my Muse
And found such fair assistance in my verse
As every alien pen hath got my use
And under thee their poesy disperse.
Thine eyes that taught the dumb on high to sing
And heavy ignorance aloft to fly,
Have added feathers to the learnèd's wing
And given grace a double majesty.
Yet be most proud of that which I compile,
Whose influence is thine and born of thee.
In others' works thou dost but mend the style,
And arts with thy sweet graces gracèd be:
    But thou art all my art and dost advance
    As high as learning my rude ignorance.

Sonnet 79

Whilst I alone did call upon thy aid,
My verse alone had all thy gentle grace,
But now my gracious numbers are decayed
And my sick Muse doth give another place.
I grant, sweet love, thy lovely argument
Deserves the travail of a worthier pen,
Yet what of thee thy poet doth invent
He robs thee of and pays it thee again.
He lends thee virtue and he stole that word
From thy behaviour, beauty doth he give
And found it in thy cheek: he can afford
No praise to thee but what in thee doth live.
    Then thank him not for that which he doth say,
    Since what he owes thee thou thyself dost pay.

Sonnet 80

O, how I faint when I of you do write,
Knowing a better spirit doth use your name
And in the praise thereof spends all his might
To make me tongue-tied, speaking of your fame.
But since your worth, wide as the ocean is,
The humble as the proudest sail doth bear,
My saucy bark inferior far to his
On your broad main doth wilfully appear.
Your shallowest help will hold me up afloat,
Whilst he upon your soundless deep doth ride,
Or being wrecked, I am a worthless boat,
He of tall building and of goodly pride.
    Then if he thrive and I be cast away,
    The worst was this: my love was my decay.

Sonnet 81

Or I shall live your epitaph to make,
Or you survive when I in earth am rotten,
From hence your memory death cannot take,
Although in me each part will be forgotten.
Your name from hence immortal life shall have,
Though I, once gone, to all the world must die.
The earth can yield me but a common grave,
When you entombèd in men's eyes shall lie.
Your monument shall be my gentle verse,
Which eyes not yet created shall o'er-read,
And tongues to be your being shall rehearse
When all the breathers of this world are dead.
    You still shall live — such virtue hath my pen —
    Where breath most breathes, ev'n in the mouths of men.

Sonnet 82

I grant thou wert not married to my Muse
And therefore mayst without attaint o'erlook
The dedicated words which writers use
Of their fair subject, blessing every book.
Thou art as fair in knowledge as in hue,
Finding thy worth a limit past my praise,
And therefore art enforced to seek anew
Some fresher stamp of the time-bett'ring days.
And do so, love, yet when they have devised
What strainèd touches rhetoric can lend,
Thou, truly fair, wert truly sympathized
In true plain words by thy true-telling friend.
 And their gross painting might be better used
 Where cheeks need blood: in thee it is abused.

Sonnet 83

I never saw that you did painting need,
And therefore to your fair no painting set.
I found, or thought I found, you did exceed
The barren tender of a poet's debt,
And therefore have I slept in your report,
That you yourself being extant well might show
How far a modern quill doth come too short,
Speaking of worth, what worth in you doth grow.
This silence for my sin you did impute,
Which shall be most my glory, being dumb,
For I impair not beauty being mute,
When others would give life and bring a tomb.
   There lives more life in one of your fair eyes
   Than both your poets can in praise devise.

Sonnet 84

Who is it that says most, which can say more
Than this rich praise, that you alone are you,
In whose confine immurèd is the store
Which should example where your equal grew?
Lean penury within that pen doth dwell
That to his subject lends not some small glory,
But he that writes of you, if he can tell
That you are you, so dignifies his story.
Let him but copy what in you is writ,
Not making worse what nature made so clear,
And such a counterpart shall fame his wit,
Making his style admirèd everywhere.
   You to your beauteous blessings add a curse,
    Being fond on praise, which makes your praises worse.

Sonnet 85

My tongue-tied Muse in manners holds her still,
While comments of your praise, richly compiled,
Reserve their character with golden quill
And precious phrase by all the Muses filed.
I think good thoughts whilst other write good words,
And like unlettered clerk still cry 'Amen'
To every hymn that able spirit affords
In polished form of well-refinèd pen.
Hearing you praised, I say, ''Tis so, 'tis true',
And to the most of praise add something more:
But that is in my thought, whose love to you,
Though words come hindmost, holds his rank before.
    Then others for the breath of words respect,
    Me for my dumb thoughts, speaking in effect.

Sonnet 86

Was it the proud full sail of his great verse,
Bound for the prize of all-too-precious you,
That did my ripe thoughts in my brain inhearse,
Making their tomb the womb wherein they grew?
Was it his spirit, by spirits taught to write
Above a mortal pitch, that struck me dead?
No, neither he nor his compeers by night
Giving him aid, my verse astonishèd.
He, nor that affable familiar ghost
Which nightly gulls him with intelligence,
As victors of my silence cannot boast.
I was not sick of any fear from thence,
   But when your countenance filled up his line,
   Then lacked I matter, that enfeebled mine.

Sonnet 87

Farewell, thou art too dear for my possessing,
And like enough thou know'st thy estimate.
The charter of thy worth gives thee releasing,
My bonds in thee are all determinate.
For how do I hold thee but by thy granting?
And for that riches where is my deserving?
The cause of this fair gift in me is wanting,
And so my patent back again is swerving.
Thyself thou gav'st, thy own worth then not knowing,
Or me, to whom thou gav'st it, else mistaking;
So thy great gift, upon misprision growing,
Comes home again, on better judgement making.
    Thus have I had thee as a dream doth flatter:
    In sleep a king, but waking no such matter.

Sonnet 88

When thou shalt be disposed to set me light
And place my merit in the eye of scorn,
Upon thy side against myself I'll fight
And prove thee virtuous, though thou art forsworn.
With mine own weakness being best acquainted,
Upon thy part I can set down a story
Of faults concealed, wherein I am attainted,
That thou in losing me shalt win much glory:
And I by this will be a gainer too,
For bending all my loving thoughts on thee,
The injuries that to myself I do,
Doing thee vantage, double-vantage me.
    Such is my love, to thee I so belong,
    That for thy right myself will bear all wrong.

Sonnet 89

Say that thou didst forsake me for some fault
And I will comment upon that offence,
Speak of my lameness and I straight will halt,
Against thy reasons making no defence.
Thou canst not, love, disgrace me half so ill,
To set a form upon desirèd change,
As I'll myself disgrace, knowing thy will,
I will acquaintance strangle and look strange,
Be absent from thy walks, and in my tongue
Thy sweet belovèd name no more shall dwell,
Lest I, too much profane, should do it wrong
And haply of our old acquaintance tell.
   For thee, against myself I'll vow debate,
   For I must ne'er love him whom thou dost hate.

Sonnet 90

Then hate me when thou wilt, if ever, now,
Now, while the world is bent my deeds to cross,
Join with the spite of fortune, make me bow,
And do not drop in for an after-loss.
Ah do not, when my heart hath scaped this sorrow,
Come in the rearward of a conquered woe,
Give not a windy night a rainy morrow
To linger out a purposed overthrow.
If thou wilt leave me, do not leave me last,
When other petty griefs have done their spite,
But in the onset come: so shall I taste
At first the very worst of fortune's might,
    And other strains of woe, which now seem woe,
    Compared with loss of thee will not seem so.

Sonnet 91

Some glory in their birth, some in their skill,
Some in their wealth, some in their body's force,
Some in their garments, though new-fangled ill,
Some in their hawks and hounds, some in their horse,
And every humour hath his adjunct pleasure,
Wherein it finds a joy above the rest,
But these particulars are not my measure:
All these I better in one general best.
Thy love is better than high birth to me,
Richer than wealth, prouder than garments' cost,
Of more delight than hawks or horses be:
And having thee, of all men's pride I boast —
    Wretched in this alone, that thou mayst take
    All this away and me most wretched make.

Sonnet 92

But do thy worst to steal thyself away,
For term of life thou art assurèd mine,
And life no longer than thy love will stay,
For it depends upon that love of thine.
Then need I not to fear the worst of wrongs,
When in the least of them my life hath end.
I see a better state to me belongs
Than that which on thy humour doth depend.
Thou canst not vex me with inconstant mind,
Since that my life on thy revolt doth lie.
O, what a happy title do I find,
Happy to have thy love, happy to die.
    But what's so blessèd-fair that fears no blot?
    Thou mayst be false, and yet I know it not.

Sonnet 93

So shall I live, supposing thou art true,
Like a deceivèd husband: so love's face
May still seem love to me, though altered new,
Thy looks with me, thy heart in other place,
For there can live no hatred in thine eye,
Therefore in that I cannot know thy change.
In many's looks the false heart's history
Is writ in moods and frowns and wrinkles strange,
But heaven in thy creation did decree
That in thy face sweet love should ever dwell.
Whate'er thy thoughts or thy heart's workings be,
Thy looks should nothing thence but sweetness tell.
   How like Eve's apple doth thy beauty grow,
   If thy sweet virtue answer not thy show.

Sonnet 94

They that have power to hurt and will do none,
That do not do the thing they most do show,
Who, moving others, are themselves as stone,
Unmovèd, cold, and to temptation slow:
They rightly do inherit heaven's graces
And husband nature's riches from expense.
They are the lords and owners of their faces,
Others but stewards of their excellence.
The summer's flower is to the summer sweet,
Though to itself it only live and die,
But if that flower with base infection meet,
The basest weed outbraves his dignity:
    For sweetest things turn sourest by their deeds,
    Lilies that fester smell far worse than weeds.

Sonnet 95

How sweet and lovely dost thou make the shame
Which, like a canker in the fragrant rose,
Doth spot the beauty of thy budding name.
O, in what sweets dost thou thy sins enclose!
That tongue that tells the story of thy days,
Making lascivious comments on thy sport,
Cannot dispraise but in a kind of praise:
Naming thy name blesses an ill report.
O, what a mansion have those vices got
Which for their habitation chose out thee,
Where beauty's veil doth cover every blot,
And all things turns to fair that eyes can see.
    Take heed, dear heart, of this large privilege:
    The hardest knife ill-used doth lose his edge.

Sonnet 96

Some say thy fault is youth, some wantonness,
Some say thy grace is youth and gentle sport,
Both grace and faults are loved of more and less:
Thou mak'st faults graces that to thee resort.
As on the finger of a thronèd queen
The basest jewel will be well esteemed,
So are those errors that in thee are seen
To truths translated and for true things deemed.
How many lambs might the stern wolf betray,
If like a lamb he could his looks translate?
How many gazers mightst thou lead away,
If thou wouldst use the strength of all thy state?
   But do not so: I love thee in such sort
    As, thou being mine, mine is thy good report.

Sonnet 97

How like a winter hath my absence been
From thee, the pleasure of the fleeting year.
What freezings have I felt, what dark days seen,
What old December's bareness everywhere.
And yet this time removed was summer's time,
The teeming autumn, big with rich increase,
Bearing the wanton burden of the prime,
Like widowed wombs after their lords' decease:
Yet this abundant issue seemed to me
But hope of orphans and unfathered fruit,
For summer and his pleasures wait on thee,
And, thou away, the very birds are mute —
    Or if they sing, 'tis with so dull a cheer
    That leaves look pale, dreading the winter's near.

Sonnet 98

From you have I been absent in the spring,
When proud-pied April dressed in all his trim
Hath put a spirit of youth in everything,
That heavy Saturn laughed and leaped with him.
Yet nor the lays of birds nor the sweet smell
Of different flowers in odour and in hue
Could make me any summer's story tell,
Or from their proud lap pluck them where they grew.
Nor did I wonder at the lily's white,
Nor praise the deep vermilion in the rose.
They were but sweet, but figures of delight,
Drawn after you, you pattern of all those.
    Yet seemed it winter still and, you away,
    As with your shadow I with these did play.

Sonnet 99

The forward violet thus did I chide:
Sweet thief, whence didst thou steal thy sweet that
    smells,
If not from my love's breath? The purple pride
Which on thy soft cheek for complexion dwells
In my love's veins thou hast too grossly dyed.
The lily I condemnèd for thy hand,
And buds of marjoram had stol'n thy hair:
The roses fearfully on thorns did stand,
One blushing shame, another white despair,
A third, nor red nor white, had stol'n of both
And to his robb'ry had annexed thy breath:
But for his theft, in pride of all his growth,
A vengeful canker eat him up to death.
    More flowers I noted, yet I none could see
    But sweet or colour it had stol'n from thee.

Sonnet 100

Where art thou, Muse, that thou forget'st so long
To speak of that which gives thee all thy might?
Spend'st thou thy fury on some worthless song,
Dark'ning thy power to lend base subjects light?
Return, forgetful Muse, and straight redeem
In gentle numbers time so idly spent,
Sing to the ear that doth thy lays esteem
And gives thy pen both skill and argument.
Rise, resty Muse, my love's sweet face survey,
If Time have any wrinkle graven there,
If any, be a satire to decay
And make Time's spoils despisèd everywhere.
  Give my love fame faster than Time wastes life,
  So thou prevent'st his scythe and crooked knife.

Sonnet 101

O truant Muse, what shall be thy amends
For thy neglect of truth in beauty dyed?
Both truth and beauty on my love depends,
So dost thou too, and therein dignified.
Make answer, Muse. Wilt thou not haply say,
'Truth needs no colour, with his colour fixed,
Beauty no pencil, beauty's truth to lay,
But best is best, if never intermixed'?
Because he needs no praise, wilt thou be dumb?
Excuse not silence so, for't lies in thee
To make him much outlive a gilded tomb
And to be praised of ages yet to be.
    Then do thy office, Muse. I teach thee how
        To make him seem long hence, as he shows now.

Sonnet 102

My love is strengthened, though more weak in seeming:
I love not less, though less the show appear.
That love is merchandised whose rich esteeming
The owner's tongue doth publish everywhere.
Our love was new and then but in the spring,
When I was wont to greet it with my lays,
As Philomel in summer's front doth sing
And stops his pipe in growth of riper days:
Not that the summer is less pleasant now
Than when her mournful hymns did hush the night,
But that wild music burdens every bough,
And sweets grown common lose their dear delight.
    Therefore, like her, I sometime hold my tongue,
    Because I would not dull you with my song.

Sonnet 103

Alack, what poverty my Muse brings forth,
That having such a scope to show her pride,
The argument all bare is of more worth
Than when it hath my added praise beside.
O, blame me not, if I no more can write.
Look in your glass, and there appears a face
That overgoes my blunt invention quite,
Dulling my lines and doing me disgrace.
Were it not sinful then, striving to mend,
To mar the subject that before was well?
For to no other pass my verses tend
Than of your graces and your gifts to tell.
    And more, much more, than in my verse can sit
    Your own glass shows you when you look in it.

Sonnet 104

To me, fair friend, you never can be old,
For as you were when first your eye I eyed,
Such seems your beauty still. Three winters cold
Have from the forests shook three summers' pride,
Three beauteous springs to yellow autumn turned
In process of the seasons have I seen,
Three April perfumes in three hot Junes burned,
Since first I saw you fresh, which yet are green.
Ah yet doth beauty, like a dial hand,
Steal from his figure and no pace perceived:
So your sweet hue, which methinks still doth stand,
Hath motion and mine eye may be deceived.
　For fear of which, hear this, thou age unbred:
　Ere you were born was beauty's summer dead.

Sonnet 105

Let not my love be called idolatry,
Nor my belovèd as an idol show,
Since all alike my songs and praises be
To one, of one, still such and ever so.
Kind is my love today, tomorrow kind,
Still constant in a wondrous excellence.
Therefore my verse to constancy confined,
One thing expressing, leaves out difference.
'Fair, kind and true' is all my argument,
'Fair, kind and true' varying to other words,
And in this change is my invention spent,
Three themes in one, which wondrous scope affords.
    Fair, kind and true have often lived alone,
     Which three till now never kept seat in one.

Sonnet 106

When in the chronicle of wasted time
I see descriptions of the fairest wights,
And beauty making beautiful old rhyme
In praise of ladies dead and lovely knights,
Then in the blazon of sweet beauty's best,
Of hand, of foot, of lip, of eye, of brow,
I see their antique pen would have expressed
Even such a beauty as you master now.
So all their praises are but prophecies
Of this our time, all you prefiguring,
And, for they looked but with divining eyes,
They had not skill enough your worth to sing:
    For we, which now behold these present days,
    Have eyes to wonder, but lack tongues to praise.

Sonnet 107

Not mine own fears, nor the prophetic soul
Of the wide world dreaming on things to come,
Can yet the lease of my true love control,
Supposed as forfeit to a confined doom.
The mortal moon hath her eclipse endured
And the sad augurs mock their own presage,
Incertainties now crown themselves assured
And peace proclaims olives of endless age.
Now with the drops of this most balmy time
My love looks fresh and Death to me subscribes,
Since, spite of him, I'll live in this poor rhyme,
While he insults o'er dull and speechless tribes.
  And thou in this shalt find thy monument,
    When tyrants' crests and tombs of brass are spent.

Sonnet 108

What's in the brain that ink may character
Which hath not figured to thee my true spirit?
What's new to speak, what now to register,
That may express my love or thy dear merit?
Nothing, sweet boy, but yet like prayers divine
I must each day say o'er the very same,
Counting no old thing old, thou mine, I thine,
Even as when first I hallowed thy fair name.
So that eternal love in love's fresh case
Weighs not the dust and injury of age,
Nor gives to necessary wrinkles place,
But makes antiquity for aye his page,
    Finding the first conceit of love there bred,
    Where time and outward form would show it dead.

Sonnet 109

O, never say that I was false of heart,
Though absence seemed my flame to qualify.
As easy might I from myself depart
As from my soul, which in thy breast doth lie:
That is my home of love. If I have ranged,
Like him that travels I return again,
Just to the time, not with the time exchanged,
So that myself bring water for my stain.
Never believe, though in my nature reigned
All frailties that besiege all kinds of blood,
That it could so preposterously be stained,
To leave for nothing all thy sum of good:
    For nothing this wide universe I call,
      Save thou, my rose — in it thou art my all.

Sonnet 110

Alas, 'tis true, I have gone here and there
And made myself a motley to the view,
Gored mine own thoughts, sold cheap what is most dear,
Made old offences of affections new.
Most true it is that I have looked on truth
Askance and strangely, but, by all above,
These blenches gave my heart another youth,
And worse essays proved thee my best of love.
Now all is done, have what shall have no end:
Mine appetite I never more will grind
On newer proof, to try an older friend,
A god in love, to whom I am confined.
   Then give me welcome, next my heaven the best,
   Even to thy pure and most most loving breast.

Sonnet 111

O, for my sake do you with Fortune chide,
The guilty goddess of my harmful deeds,
That did not better for my life provide
Than public means which public manners breeds.
Thence comes it that my name receives a brand,
And almost thence my nature is subdued
To what it works in, like the dyer's hand.
Pity me then and wish I were renewed,
Whilst, like a willing patient, I will drink
Potions of eisel gainst my strong infection,
No bitterness that I will bitter think,
Nor double penance to correct correction.
    Pity me then, dear friend, and I assure ye
    Even that your pity is enough to cure me.

Sonnet 112

Your love and pity doth th'impression fill
Which vulgar scandal stamped upon my brow,
For what care I who calls me well or ill,
So you o'er-green my bad, my good allow?
You are my all the world and I must strive
To know my shames and praises from your tongue.
None else to me, nor I to none alive,
That my steeled sense or changes right or wrong.
In so profound abysm I throw all care
Of others' voices, that my adder's sense
To critic and to flatterer stoppèd are.
Mark how with my neglect I do dispense:
    You are so strongly in my purpose bred
    That all the world besides me thinks you're dead.

Sonnet 113

Since I left you, mine eye is in my mind,
And that which governs me to go about
Doth part his function and is partly blind,
Seems seeing, but effectually is out,
For it no form delivers to the heart
Of bird, of flower, or shape which it doth latch.
Of his quick objects hath the mind no part,
Nor his own vision holds what it doth catch,
For if it see the rud'st or gentlest sight,
The most sweet favour or deformed'st creature,
The mountain or the sea, the day or night,
The crow or dove, it shapes them to your feature.
    Incapable of more, replete with you,
    My most true mind thus makes mine eye untrue.

Sonnet 114

Or whether doth my mind, being crowned with you,
Drink up the monarch's plague, this flattery?
Or whether shall I say mine eye saith true,
And that your love taught it this alchemy,
To make of monsters and things indigest
Such cherubins as your sweet self resemble,
Creating every bad a perfect best,
As fast as objects to his beams assemble?
O, 'tis the first, 'tis flatt'ry in my seeing,
And my great mind most kingly drinks it up:
Mine eye well knows what with his gust is 'greeing,
And to his palate doth prepare the cup.
    If it be poisoned, 'tis the lesser sin
    That mine eye loves it and doth first begin.

Sonnet 115

Those lines that I before have writ do lie,
Even those that said I could not love you dearer:
Yet then my judgement knew no reason why
My most full flame should afterwards burn clearer.
But reckoning time, whose millioned accidents
Creep in 'twixt vows and change decrees of kings,
Tan sacred beauty, blunt the sharp'st intents,
Divert strong minds to th'course of alt'ring things —
Alas why, fearing of Time's tyranny,
Might I not then say, 'Now I love you best',
When I was certain o'er incertainty,
Crowning the present, doubting of the rest?
    Love is a babe: then might I not say so,
    To give full growth to that which still doth grow?

Sonnet 116

Let me not to the marriage of true minds
Admit impediments. Love is not love
Which alters when it alteration finds
Or bends with the remover to remove.
O no, it is an ever-fixèd mark
That looks on tempests and is never shaken,
It is the star to every wand'ring bark,
Whose worth's unknown, although his height be taken.
Love's not Time's fool, though rosy lips and cheeks
Within his bending sickle's compass come:
Love alters not with his brief hours and weeks,
But bears it out even to the edge of doom.
   If this be error and upon me proved,
   I never writ, nor no man ever loved.

Sonnet 117

Accuse me thus: that I have scanted all
Wherein I should your great deserts repay,
Forgot upon your dearest love to call,
Whereto all bonds do tie me day by day,
That I have frequent been with unknown minds
And given to time your own dear-purchased right,
That I have hoisted sail to all the winds
Which should transport me farthest from your sight.
Book both my wilfulness and errors down,
And on just proof surmise, accumulate,
Bring me within the level of your frown,
But shoot not at me in your wakened hate,
    Since my appeal says I did strive to prove
    The constancy and virtue of your love.

Sonnet 118

Like as to make our appetites more keen
With eager compounds we our palate urge,
As to prevent our maladies unseen
We sicken to shun sickness when we purge,
Even so, being full of your ne'er-cloying sweetness,
To bitter sauces did I frame my feeding
And, sick of welfare, found a kind of meetness
To be diseased ere that there was true needing.
Thus policy in love, t'anticipate
The ills that were not, grew to faults assured
And brought to medicine a healthful state
Which, rank of goodness, would by ill be cured.
    But thence I learn and find the lesson true,
    Drugs poison him that so fell sick of you.

Sonnet 119

What potions have I drunk of siren tears,
Distilled from limbecks foul as hell within,
Applying fears to hopes and hopes to fears,
Still losing when I saw myself to win?
What wretched errors hath my heart committed,
Whilst it hath thought itself so blessèd never?
How have mine eyes out of their spheres been fitted
In the distraction of this madding fever?
O benefit of ill, now I find true
That better is by evil still made better,
And ruined love, when it is built anew,
Grows fairer than at first, more strong, far greater.
    So I return rebuked to my content
    And gain by ills thrice more than I have spent.

Sonnet 120

That you were once unkind befriends me now,
And for that sorrow which I then did feel
Needs must I under my transgression bow,
Unless my nerves were brass or hammered steel.
For if you were by my unkindness shaken
As I by yours, you've passed a hell of time,
And I, a tyrant, have no leisure taken
To weigh how once I suffered in your crime.
O, that our night of woe might have remembered
My deepest sense how hard true sorrow hits,
And soon to you, as you to me then, tendered
The humble salve which wounded bosoms fits.
　　But that your trespass now becomes a fee:
　　Mine ransoms yours and yours must ransom me.

Sonnet 121

'Tis better to be vile than vile esteemed,
When not to be receives reproach of being,
And the just pleasure lost which is so deemed
Not by our feeling but by others' seeing.
For why should others' false adulterate eyes
Give salutation to my sportive blood?
Or on my frailties why are frailer spies,
Which in their wills count bad what I think good?
No, I am that I am and they that level
At my abuses reckon up their own:
I may be straight, though they themselves be bevel.
By their rank thoughts my deeds must not be shown,
   Unless this general evil they maintain:
   All men are bad and in their badness reign.

Sonnet 122

Thy gift, thy tables, are within my brain
Full charactered with lasting memory,
Which shall above that idle rank remain
Beyond all date, even to eternity,
Or at the least, so long as brain and heart
Have faculty by nature to subsist,
Till each to razed oblivion yield his part
Of thee, thy record never can be missed.
That poor retention could not so much hold,
Nor need I tallies thy dear love to score.
Therefore to give them from me was I bold,
To trust those tables that receive thee more.
   To keep an adjunct to remember thee
   Were to import forgetfulness in me.

Sonnet 123

No, Time, thou shalt not boast that I do change.
Thy pyramids built up with newer might
To me are nothing novel, nothing strange:
They are but dressings of a former sight.
Our dates are brief and therefore we admire
What thou dost foist upon us that is old,
And rather make them born to our desire
Than think that we before have heard them told.
Thy registers and thee I both defy,
Not wond'ring at the present nor the past,
For thy records and what we see doth lie,
Made more or less by thy continual haste.
   This I do vow and this shall ever be:
   I will be true, despite thy scythe and thee.

Sonnet 124

If my dear love were but the child of state,
It might for Fortune's bastard be unfathered,
As subject to time's love or to time's hate,
Weeds among weeds, or flowers with flowers gathered.
No, it was builded far from accident,
It suffers not in smiling pomp, nor falls
Under the blow of thrallèd discontent,
Whereto th'inviting time our fashion calls.
It fears not policy, that heretic,
Which works on leases of short-numbered hours,
But all alone stands hugely politic,
That it nor grows with heat nor drowns with showers.
    To this I witness call the fools of time,
      Which die for goodness, who have lived for crime.

Sonnet 125

Were't aught to me I bore the canopy,
With my extern the outward honouring,
Or laid great bases for eternity,
Which proves more short than waste or ruining?
Have I not seen dwellers on form and favour
Lose all and more, by paying too much rent,
For compound sweet forgoing simple savour,
Pitiful thrivers, in their gazing spent?
No, let me be obsequious in thy heart,
And take thou my oblation, poor but free,
Which is not mixed with seconds, knows no art,
But mutual render, only me for thee.
   Hence, thou suborned informer, a true soul
   When most impeached stands least in thy control.

Sonnet 126

O thou, my lovely boy, who in thy power
Dost hold Time's fickle glass, his sickle hour,
Who hast by waning grown, and therein show'st
Thy lovers withering as thy sweet self grow'st —
If Nature, sovereign mistress over wrack,
As thou goest onwards, still will pluck thee back,
She keeps thee to this purpose, that her skill
May Time disgrace and wretched minutes kill.
Yet fear her, O thou minion of her pleasure:
She may detain, but not still keep, her treasure.
Her audit, though delayed, answered must be,
And her quietus is to render thee.

   (   )
   (   )

Sonnet 127

In the old age black was not counted fair,
Or if it were, it bore not beauty's name.
But now is black beauty's successive heir
And beauty slandered with a bastard shame:
For since each hand hath put on nature's power,
Fairing the foul with art's false borrowed face,
Sweet beauty hath no name, no holy bower,
But is profaned, if not lives in disgrace.
Therefore my mistress' brows are raven black,
Her eyes so suited, and they mourners seem
At such who, not born fair, no beauty lack,
Sland'ring creation with a false esteem.
    Yet so they mourn, becoming of their woe,
      That every tongue says beauty should look so.

Sonnet 128

How oft, when thou, my music, music play'st
Upon that blessèd wood whose motion sounds
With thy sweet fingers, when thou gently sway'st
The wiry concord that mine ear confounds,
Do I envy those jacks that nimble leap
To kiss the tender inward of thy hand,
Whilst my poor lips, which should that harvest reap,
At the wood's boldness by thee blushing stand.
To be so tickled, they would change their state
And situation with those dancing chips
O'er whom thy fingers walk with gentle gait,
Making dead wood more blest than living lips.
    Since saucy jacks so happy are in this,
    Give them thy fingers, me thy lips to kiss.

Sonnet 129

Th'expense of spirit in a waste of shame
Is lust in action, and till action, lust
Is perjured, murd'rous, bloody, full of blame,
Savage, extreme, rude, cruel, not to trust,
Enjoyed no sooner but despisèd straight,
Past reason hunted and, no sooner had,
Past reason hated as a swallowed bait
On purpose laid to make the taker mad,
Mad in pursuit and in possession so,
Had, having and in quest to have, extreme,
A bliss in proof and proved a very woe,
Before, a joy proposed — behind, a dream.
    All this the world well knows, yet none knows well
    To shun the heaven that leads men to this hell.

Sonnet 130

My mistress' eyes are nothing like the sun,
Coral is far more red than her lips' red,
If snow be white, why then her breasts are dun,
If hairs be wires, black wires grow on her head.
I have seen roses damasked, red and white,
But no such roses see I in her cheeks,
And in some perfumes is there more delight
Than in the breath that from my mistress reeks.
I love to hear her speak, yet well I know
That music hath a far more pleasing sound.
I grant I never saw a goddess go:
My mistress when she walks treads on the ground.
    And yet, by heaven, I think my love as rare
    As any she belied with false compare.

Sonnet 131

Thou art as tyrannous, so as thou art,
As those whose beauties proudly make them cruel,
For well thou know'st to my dear doting heart
Thou art the fairest and most precious jewel.
Yet in good faith some say, that thee behold,
Thy face hath not the power to make love groan.
To say they err I dare not be so bold,
Although I swear it to myself alone.
And to be sure that is not false I swear
A thousand groans but thinking on thy face
One on another's neck do witness bear
Thy black is fairest in my judgement's place.
  In nothing art thou black save in thy deeds,
  And thence this slander as I think proceeds.

Sonnet 132

Thine eyes I love and they, as pitying me,
Knowing thy heart torment me with disdain,
Have put on black and loving mourners be,
Looking with pretty ruth upon my pain.
And truly not the morning sun of heaven
Better becomes the grey cheeks of the east,
Nor that full star that ushers in the even
Doth half that glory to the sober west,
As those two mourning eyes become thy face:
O, let it then as well beseem thy heart
To mourn for me, since mourning doth thee grace,
And suit thy pity like in every part.
   Then will I swear beauty herself is black,
   And all they foul that thy complexion lack.

Sonnet 133

Beshrew that heart that makes my heart to groan
For that deep wound it gives my friend and me.
Is't not enough to torture me alone,
But slave to slavery my sweet'st friend must be?
Me from myself thy cruel eye hath taken,
And my next self thou harder hast engrossed.
Of him, myself and thee, I am forsaken,
A torment thrice threefold thus to be crossed.
Prison my heart in thy steel bosom's ward,
But then my friend's heart let my poor heart bail,
Whoe'er keeps me, let my heart be his guard:
Thou canst not then use rigour in my jail.
   And yet thou wilt, for I, being pent in thee,
    Perforce am thine and all that is in me.

Sonnet 134

So, now I have confessed that he is thine,
And I myself am mortgaged to thy will,
Myself I'll forfeit, so that other mine
Thou wilt restore, to be my comfort still:
But thou wilt not, nor he will not be free,
For thou art covetous and he is kind.
He learned but surety-like to write for me
Under that bond that him as fast doth bind.
The statute of thy beauty thou wilt take,
Thou usurer, that put'st forth all to use,
And sue a friend came debtor for my sake:
So him I lose through my unkind abuse.
  Him have I lost, thou hast both him and me:
  He pays the whole, and yet am I not free.

Sonnet 135

Whoever hath her wish, thou hast thy Will,
And Will to boot, and Will in overplus:
More than enough am I that vex thee still,
To thy sweet will making addition thus.
Wilt thou, whose will is large and spacious,
Not once vouchsafe to hide my will in thine?
Shall will in others seem right gracious,
And in my will no fair acceptance shine?
The sea all water, yet receives rain still
And in abundance addeth to his store.
So thou, being rich in Will, add to thy Will
One will of mine, to make thy large Will more.
   Let no unkind, no fair beseechers kill:
   Think all but one and me in that one Will.

Sonnet 136

If thy soul check thee that I come so near,
Swear to thy blind soul that I was thy Will,
And will, thy soul knows, is admitted there:
Thus far for love my love-suit, sweet, fulfil.
Will will fulfil the treasure of thy love,
Ay, fill it full with wills, and my will one.
In things of great receipt with ease we prove
Among a number one is reckoned none.
Then in the number let me pass untold,
Though in thy store's account I one must be:
For nothing hold me, so it please thee hold
That nothing me, a something sweet to thee.
    Make but my name thy love and love that still,
    And then thou lovest me, for my name is Will.

Sonnet 137

Thou blind fool, love, what dost thou to mine eyes,
That they behold and see not what they see?
They know what beauty is, see where it lies,
Yet what the best is take the worst to be.
If eyes corrupt by over-partial looks
Be anchored in the bay where all men ride,
Why of eyes' falsehood hast thou forgèd hooks,
Whereto the judgement of my heart is tied?
Why should my heart think that a several plot
Which my heart knows the wide world's common place?
Or mine eyes seeing this, say this is not,
To put fair truth upon so foul a face?
   In things right true my heart and eyes have erred,
   And to this false plague are they now transferred.

Sonnet 138

When my love swears that she is made of truth,
I do believe her, though I know she lies,
That she might think me some untutored youth,
Unlearnèd in the world's false subtleties.
Thus vainly thinking that she thinks me young,
Although she knows my days are past the best,
Simply I credit her false-speaking tongue:
On both sides thus is simple truth suppressed.
But wherefore says she not she is unjust?
And wherefore say not I that I am old?
O, love's best habit is in seeming trust,
And age in love loves not to have years told.
  Therefore I lie with her and she with me,
  And in our faults by lies we flattered be.

Sonnet 139

O, call not me to justify the wrong
That thy unkindness lays upon my heart,
Wound me not with thine eye but with thy tongue,
Use power with power and slay me not by art,
Tell me thou lov'st elsewhere, but in my sight,
Dear heart, forbear to glance thine eye aside.
What need'st thou wound with cunning when thy might
Is more than my o'erpressed defence can bide?
Let me excuse thee: ah, my love well knows
Her pretty looks have been mine enemies,
And therefore from my face she turns my foes,
That they elsewhere might dart their injuries:
    Yet do not so, but since I am near slain,
    Kill me outright with looks and rid my pain.

Sonnet 140

Be wise as thou art cruel, do not press
My tongue-tied patience with too much disdain,
Lest sorrow lend me words and words express
The manner of my pity-wanting pain.
If I might teach thee wit, better it were,
Though not to love, yet, love, to tell me so,
As testy sick men, when their deaths be near,
No news but health from their physicians know.
For if I should despair, I should grow mad,
And in my madness might speak ill of thee.
Now this ill-wresting world is grown so bad,
Mad slanderers by mad ears believèd be.
    That I may not be so, nor thou belied,
        Bear thine eyes straight, though thy proud heart go wide.

Sonnet 141

In faith, I do not love thee with mine eyes,
For they in thee a thousand errors note,
But 'tis my heart that loves what they despise,
Who in despite of view is pleased to dote.
Nor are mine ears with thy tongue's tune delighted,
Nor tender feeling to base touches prone,
Nor taste, nor smell, desire to be invited
To any sensual feast with thee alone.
But my five wits nor my five senses can
Dissuade one foolish heart from serving thee,
Who leaves unswayed the likeness of a man,
Thy proud heart's slave and vassal wretch to be:
    Only my plague thus far I count my gain,
    That she that makes me sin awards me pain.

Sonnet 142

Love is my sin and thy dear virtue hate,
Hate of my sin, grounded on sinful loving.
O, but with mine compare thou thine own state,
And thou shalt find it merits not reproving,
Or if it do, not from those lips of thine
That have profaned their scarlet ornaments
And sealed false bonds of love as oft as mine,
Robbed others' beds' revenues of their rents.
Be it lawful I love thee, as thou lov'st those
Whom thine eyes woo as mine importune thee.
Root pity in thy heart, that when it grows,
Thy pity may deserve to pitied be.
   If thou dost seek to have what thou dost hide,
    By self-example mayst thou be denied.

Sonnet 143

Lo, as a careful housewife runs to catch
One of her feathered creatures broke away,
Sets down her babe and makes all swift dispatch
In pursuit of the thing she would have stay,
Whilst her neglected child holds her in chase,
Cries to catch her whose busy care is bent
To follow that which flies before her face,
Not prizing her poor infant's discontent:
So runn'st thou after that which flies from thee,
Whilst I, thy babe, chase thee afar behind.
But if thou catch thy hope, turn back to me,
And play the mother's part, kiss me, be kind.
 So will I pray that thou mayst have thy Will,
 If thou turn back and my loud crying still.

Sonnet 144

Two loves I have of comfort and despair,
Which like two spirits do suggest me still:
The better angel is a man right fair,
The worser spirit a woman coloured ill.
To win me soon to hell, my female evil
Tempteth my better angel from my side
And would corrupt my saint to be a devil,
Wooing his purity with her foul pride.
And whether that my angel be turned fiend
Suspect I may, yet not directly tell;
But being both from me, both to each friend,
I guess one angel in another's hell.
    Yet this shall I ne'er know, but live in doubt,
    Till my bad angel fire my good one out.

Sonnet 145

Those lips that Love's own hand did make
Breathed forth the sound that said 'I hate'
To me that languished for her sake.
But when she saw my woeful state,
Straight in her heart did mercy come,
Chiding that tongue that ever sweet
Was used in giving gentle doom,
And taught it thus anew to greet:
'I hate' she altered with an end
That followed it as gentle day
Doth follow night, who like a fiend
From heaven to hell is flown away.
   'I hate' from hate away she threw
   And saved my life, saying 'not you'.

Sonnet 146

Poor soul, the centre of my sinful earth,
[   ] these rebel powers that thee array,
Why dost thou pine within and suffer dearth,
Painting thy outward walls so costly gay?
Why so large cost, having so short a lease,
Dost thou upon thy fading mansion spend?
Shall worms, inheritors of this excess,
Eat up thy charge? Is this thy body's end?
Then, soul, live thou upon thy servant's loss
And let that pine to aggravate thy store,
Buy terms divine in selling hours of dross,
Within be fed, without be rich no more:
    So shalt thou feed on death, that feeds on men,
    And death once dead, there's no more dying then.

Sonnet 147

My love is as a fever, longing still
For that which longer nurseth the disease,
Feeding on that which doth preserve the ill,
Th'uncertain sickly appetite to please.
My reason, the physician to my love,
Angry that his prescriptions are not kept,
Hath left me and I desperate now approve
Desire is death, which physic did except.
Past cure I am, now reason is past care;
And frantic-mad with evermore unrest,
My thoughts and my discourse as madmen's are,
At random from the truth vainly expressed.
　　For I have sworn thee fair and thought thee bright,
　　Who art as black as hell, as dark as night.

Sonnet 148

O me, what eyes hath love put in my head,

Which have no correspondence with true sight,

Or if they have, where is my judgement fled

That censures falsely what they see aright?

If that be fair whereon my false eyes dote,

What means the world to say it is not so?

If it be not, then love doth well denote

Love's eye is not so true as all men's 'no'.

How can it? O, how can love's eye be true,

That is so vexed with watching and with tears?

No marvel then though I mistake my view:

The sun itself sees not till heaven clears.

    O cunning love, with tears thou keep'st me blind,

    Lest eyes well-seeing thy foul faults should find.

Sonnet 149

Canst thou, O cruel, say I love thee not,

When I against myself with thee partake?

Do I not think on thee, when I forgot

Am of myself, all tyrant for thy sake?

Who hateth thee that I do call my friend?

On whom frown'st thou that I do fawn upon?

Nay, if thou lour'st on me, do I not spend

Revenge upon myself with present moan?

What merit do I in myself respect,

That is so proud thy service to despise,

When all my best doth worship thy defect,

Commanded by the motion of thine eyes?

    But, love, hate on, for now I know thy mind:

    Those that can see thou lov'st, and I am blind.

Sonnet 150

O, from what power hast thou this powerful might
With insufficiency my heart to sway,
To make me give the lie to my true sight
And swear that brightness doth not grace the day?
Whence hast thou this becoming of things ill,
That in the very refuse of thy deeds
There is such strength and warrantize of skill
That in my mind thy worst all best exceeds?
Who taught thee how to make me love thee more,
The more I hear and see just cause of hate?
O, though I love what others do abhor,
With others thou shouldst not abhor my state.
  If thy unworthiness raised love in me,
  More worthy I to be beloved of thee.

Sonnet 151

Love is too young to know what conscience is,
Yet who knows not conscience is born of love?
Then, gentle cheater, urge not my amiss,
Lest guilty of my faults thy sweet self prove.
For, thou betraying me, I do betray
My nobler part to my gross body's treason.
My soul doth tell my body that he may
Triumph in love: flesh stays no further reason,
But rising at thy name doth point out thee
As his triumphant prize. Proud of this pride,
He is contented thy poor drudge to be,
To stand in thy affairs, fall by thy side.
    No want of conscience hold it that I call
    Her 'love' for whose dear love I rise and fall.

Sonnet 152

In loving thee thou know'st I am forsworn,
But thou art twice forsworn to me love swearing:
In act thy bed-vow broke and new faith torn
In vowing new hate after new love bearing.
But why of two oaths' breach do I accuse thee,
When I break twenty? I am perjured most,
For all my vows are oaths but to misuse thee,
And all my honest faith in thee is lost.
For I have sworn deep oaths of thy deep kindness,
Oaths of thy love, thy truth, thy constancy,
And to enlighten thee gave eyes to blindness,
Or made them swear against the thing they see.
　　For I have sworn thee fair: more perjured eye,
　　To swear against the truth so foul a lie.

Sonnet 153

Cupid laid by his brand and fell asleep.
A maid of Dian's this advantage found,
And his love-kindling fire did quickly steep
In a cold valley-fountain of that ground,
Which borrowed from this holy fire of love
A dateless lively heat, still to endure,
And grew a seething bath, which yet men prove
Against strange maladies a sovereign cure.
But at my mistress' eye love's brand new-fired,
The boy for trial needs would touch my breast.
I, sick withal, the help of bath desired,
And thither hied, a sad distempered guest,
    But found no cure: the bath for my help lies
    Where Cupid got new fire — my mistress' eyes.

Sonnet 154

The little Love-god lying once asleep
Laid by his side his heart-inflaming brand,
Whilst many nymphs that vowed chaste life to keep
Came tripping by, but in her maiden hand
The fairest votary took up that fire
Which many legions of true hearts had warmed,
And so the general of hot desire
Was, sleeping, by a virgin hand disarmed.
This brand she quenched in a cool well by,
Which from love's fire took heat perpetual,
Growing a bath and healthful remedy
For men diseased: but I, my mistress' thrall,
    Came there for cure, and this by that I prove:
    Love's fire heats water, water cools not love.

FINIS